Napkin Folding

44 WAYS TO TURN A SQUARE OF LINEN INTO A WORK OF ART

JAMES GINDERS

ILLUSTRATIONS BY E. R. CAPPS

HARMONY BOOKS/NEW YORK

Copyright © 1978, 1980 by James Ginders

All rights reserved. No part of this book may be reproduced or transmitted in
any form or by any means, electronic or mechanical, including photocopying,
recording, or by any information storage and retrieval system, without
permission in writing from the publisher.
Published in the United States in 1987 by Harmony Books, a division of
Crown Publishers, Inc., 225 Park Avenue South, New York, New York 10003
and represented in Canada by the Canadian MANDA Group
First published in Great Britain by DJ Costello (Publishers) Ltd.
HARMONY and colophon are trademarks of Crown Publishers, Inc.
Manufactured in the United States of America

Library of Congress Cataloging-in-Publication Data

Ginders, James.
  Napkin folding.

  1. Napkin folding. I. Title.
TX879.G56   1987   642'.7   87-7581
ISBN 0-517-56632-X (pbk.)

10 9 8 7 6 5 4 3 2

First American Edition

Contents

Introduction

Looking back through history, at the eating habits of the nobility, we find that the use of table linen began when the very rich people started to cover their dining tables with expensive decorated linen or silken drapes. The dining tables of this period tended to be long and narrow whilst the cloths were generally square; to produce the best effect, the cloths were set diagonally along the table with a corner hanging over the edge of the table in front of each diner.

The eating habits and table manners of the time did not really complement the ornate table settings, for it was common practice for the diners to wipe their greasy hands upon their clothes and to spill odds and ends of food over their somewhat extravagant clothing. This being so, it was not long before they perceived that this highly decorated cloth covering the table, with a corner so conveniently placed, could save a great deal of wear and tear on their own linen. Thus started the habit of tucking the corner of the cloth under their chins to catch the straying foodstuffs, then of course, at the end of the meal, they would wipe their dirty hands on the now bedraggled table cloth.

The laundry methods of the day were on a par with the table manners and eating habits of the nobility, so expensive cloths were soon reduced to rags, thus adding a further burden on the often delicately balanced budgets of our noble families.

It is not known who first produced the table napkins but we find them in use as early as the 15th century, when it was the fashion to tie a napkin around the neck to protect the full ruffs and laces which were worn by both sexes. From this habit, it is said, the cliché *To make both ends meet* has its roots in the old French proverb *Nover les deux bouts de sa serviette*. This may be interpreted as describing a stout gentleman trying to tie his napkin at the back of his neck.

From a plain cloth provided to protect the clothing and for cleaning the hands, the napkin has progressed up to the present time, when it has become an integral part of a well set table. In a family or informal meal setting a napkin is generally presented, smoothly rolled and slipped through a 'napkin ring', which may be of silver, ivory or bone, crested or plain. However, for formal occasions the napkin takes on a dual role, primarily to protect the diners' clothes and secondly, by skilful folding into various shapes, to enhance the decor of the table setting, or to assist in the presentation of the food – for example, the Gondola as a setting for a poached fish, the Rose for serving either bread rolls or fruit, or Cinderella's Slipper to present a flower to a lady. Coloured napkins may be used at luncheons to replace floral decorations. If a napkin carries a crest or motif it should be folded so as to display it.

Of all the necessities of life, there are a few that come before the material ones of eating and drinking. Whether we are ill or well, rich or poor, lazy or hard working, it is certain that, to live, we must eat and drink. If we are to really enjoy our food it must be well cooked and well served in a pleasing environment. So attention to detail is important, for whereas a well presented napkin will enhance a place setting, a poorly finished one will create a bad first impression on a guest.

At this time it is not known how many different types of napkin folds there are, but, by producing this book we hope to bring you pleasure and increase your repertoire.

What Mrs Beeton Said

2988. Table Napkins or 'Serviettes'

The usual size of these indispensible accompaniments to the dinner-table is either a square, measuring from 28 to 30 inches; or 28 inches in breadth, by 30 inches in length, while breakfast ones are about 24 inches square. In ordinary family use they are sometimes folded smoothly and slipped through 'napkin rings', made of bone, ivory or silver; in fact, after first using this is generally the case, each member of the family having his or her own ring. But whilst this arrangement is most convenient for family use, those required for dinner-parties and other formal occasions should be neatly and prettily folded . . . It must, however, be remembered that it is useless to attempt anything but the most simple forms unless the napkins have been slightly starched and smoothly ironed. In every case the folding must be exact, or the result will be slovenly and unsightly. A small dinner-roll, or a piece of bread cut thick, about three inches square, should be placed in each napkin . . . while, whenever it is possible to do so, the appearance of the dinner-table will be greatly improved by putting a flower or small bouquet in each napkin.

TO LAY THE CLOTH FOR DINNER

3053. According to what is to be served so must the table be laid but there are certain rules that apply equally to all. The cloth itself must first be put on straight and evenly, and if at all creased should be pressed with a clean iron over a damp cloth; next follow the decorations, and when these are complete, comes either the footman's, parlourmaid's, or housemaid's work of putting on spoons, knives, &c.

Everything necessary for laying the cloth should first be brought into the room and the serviettes be ready folded, and it is a good plan to put these round the table first, so that the same amount of space can be allowed to each person.

These occupy the spaces between the knives and forks, and in each should be put either a dinner roll (which are almost invariably used at dinner parties for a piece of bread cut rather thick) Sometimes the folding of the serviettes will also allow the introduction of a flower or tiny bouquet.

(From *The Book of Household Management* by Mrs Isabella Beeton, Ward Lock Ltd, 1898)

Do not be put off by the complicated appearance of some of the folds given in this book, they are all presented in a logical manner, which, if followed, will produce good results. Some will take a little longer than others.

To enable you to obtain the best results from folding and arranging napkins, there are some basic rules which should be observed:

1   **Hands and working surfaces should be clean.**
2   **Napkins should be spotless.**
3   **Napkins for folding should be well starched*.**
4   **Best results will be obtained if the napkins are ironed perfectly flat and square at the corners.**
     *Note: To starch napkins use a cold water starch and a hand spray. This, with a hot iron, will give the required finish.

The Napkins

The following references are given, where appropriate, at the top right of each sequence of diagrams:

Breakfast means that a breakfast napkin should be used.
Paper means that a paper napkin could be used.

The table napkin referred to throughout this book should be taken to mean the following:

The breakfast napkin .... 24 inches (60cm) square
The dinner napkin .... 26 inches (65cm) square

As a guide to the degree of intricacy one of the following appears:

Elementary
Basic
Intermediate
Advanced

1 Fold napkin into three.

2 Crease at centre line **A**.

3 Fold down corners **B** and **C** to centre line.

4 Turn napkin over.

5 Roll **D** and **E** up tightly.

6 Fold at centre line **A**, leaving **D** and **E** on the outside.

7 Holding the napkin in the left hand by the rolled sections **D** and **E**, place the right hand inside the fold and bring point **F** down through the fold to point **G**.

8 Arrange napkin as shown with the rolls on top.

The Everyday Fold

Breakfast/Paper napkin · ELEMENTARY

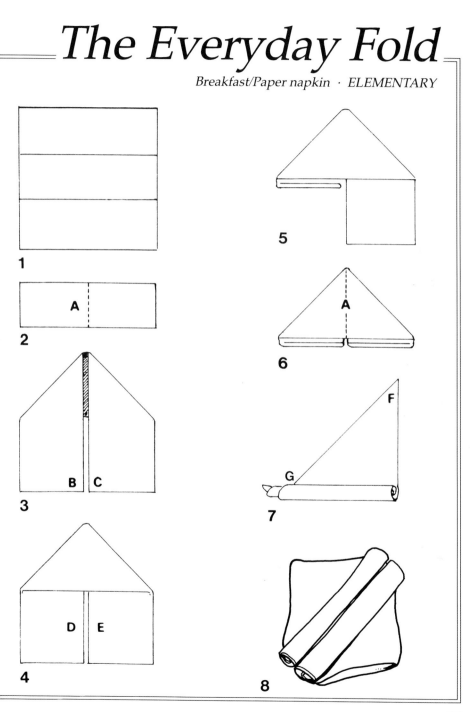

1 Lay out the napkin as a diamond. Fold in half to form a triangle.

2 Fold as indicated by the dotted line.

3 Turn so that the fold is away from you.

4 Roll the napkin inwards from the right, tucking in the end to fasten.

5 Finished Fold.

Candle

Paper napkin · ELEMENTARY

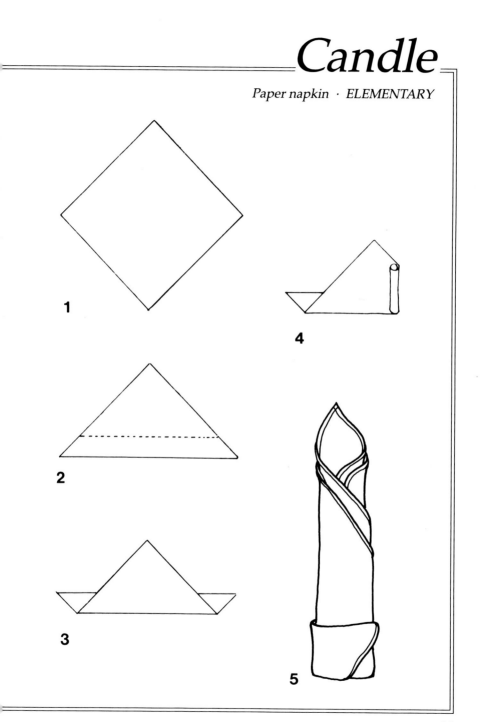

1

2

3

4

5

1   Fold the napkin in three along the dotted lines to form a rectangle. Turn the napkin so that the narrow side is towards you.

2   Fold ends **A** and **B** over along the dotted lines.

3   Fold **B** over once more.

4   Turn edge **A** over so that it meets the edge of the top fold **B**.

5   Turn edge **C** under so that **A** is now the top. Position by plate as shown.

Note: The name card or menu may be placed in between the steps of this fold.

The French Fold

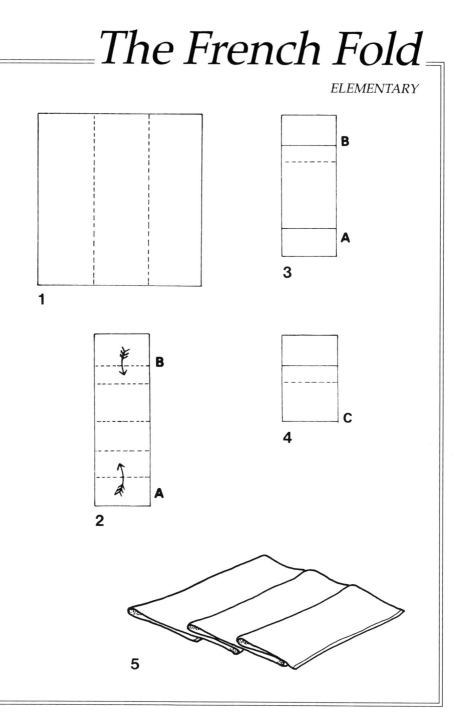

1

2

3

4

5

1 Fold the napkin into three along the dotted lines.

2 Lay both hands, palms up, on the napkin taking corner **A** between the thumb and forefinger of the left hand and corner **B** with the right hand.

3 Turn your hands palm down, retaining hold of the corners.

4 Turn your hands in towards your body in a circular motion.

5 Complete the motion, this will trap your hands.

6 Release your hands, place the napkin into a glass and arrange the leaves neatly.

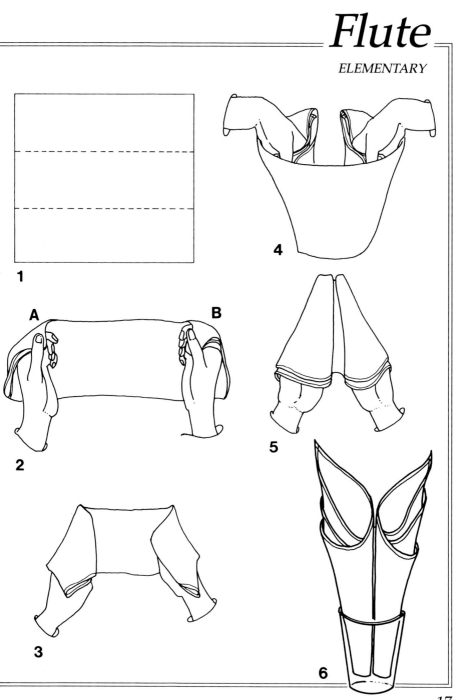

1

A   B

2

3

4

5

6

1 Fold the napkin into three.

2 Fold edges **A** to centre line **B**.

3 Fold the triangles **C** to the centre line.

4 Napkin after stage 3.

5 Take the napkin in both hands, with the points towards you and the plain side uppermost, roll to form a cone.

6 Tuck corner **A** into corner **B**.

7 Place on the table with the opening down and the points away from the diner.

The Hog's Head

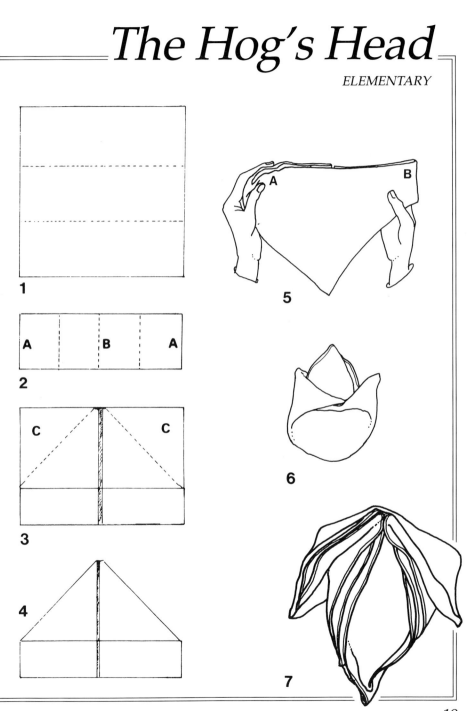

1

2

3

4

5

6

7

1 Fold the napkin into four along the dotted lines.

2 Fold the napkin in half diagonally along the dotted line. Turn the napkin so that the base **AA** is towards you.

3 Pleat the napkin from left to right.

4 Set the napkin in a wine glass, open out the pleats and arrange as shown.

Paper napkin · ELEMENTARY

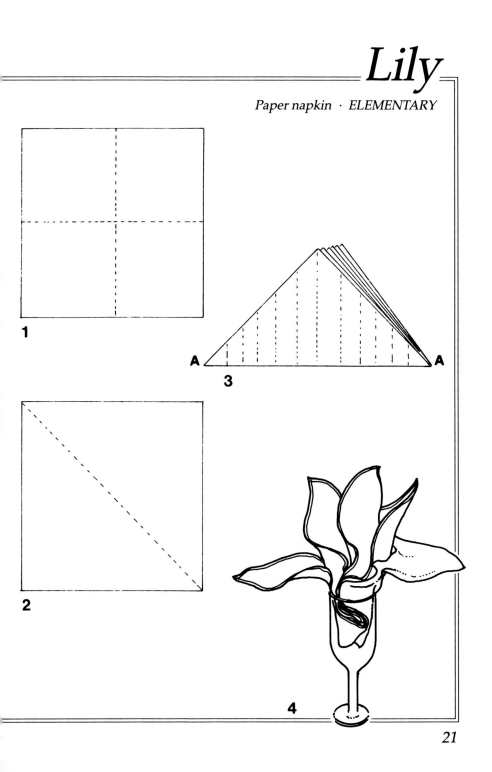

1

2

3

A — A

4

1   Fold the napkin in three as shown.

2   Fold edges **A** to centre line **B**.

3   Fold corners **C** to centre line.

4   Napkin after stage 3.

5   Take the napkin in both hands and, with the points towards you and the plain side uppermost, roll to form a cone.

6   Tuck corner **A** into corner **B**.

7   Place on the table with the opening down and the points towards the diner.

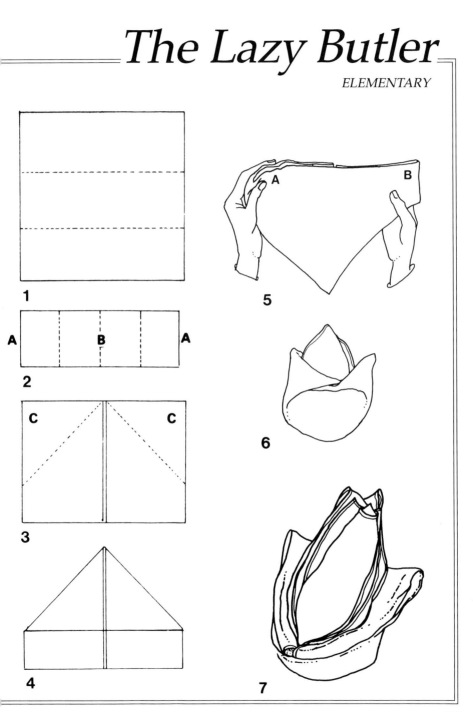

1

2

3

4

5

6

7

1 Fold the napkin into three as shown.

2 Fold at line **B** leaving about 6 inches (15cm) at end **A**.

3 Pleat from **C** to **B**.

4 Fold in half as shown.

5 Fold triangle **A** over along the dotted line; this will form a support for the finished fold. Open out the pleats and arrange as shown.

6 Finished Fold.

Rising Sun Fan

Paper napkin · ELEMENTARY

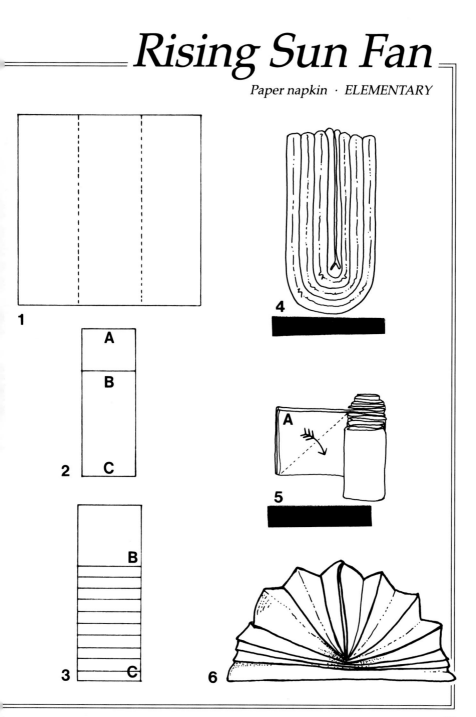

1 Lay napkin out as shown.

2 Fold to form a triangle with the points away from you.

3 Roll tightly from the base to within 2½ inches (6.5cm) from the top.

4 Fold in half as shown, and set on a side plate.

5 Finished Fold.

The Sail Boat

Paper napkin · *ELEMENTARY*

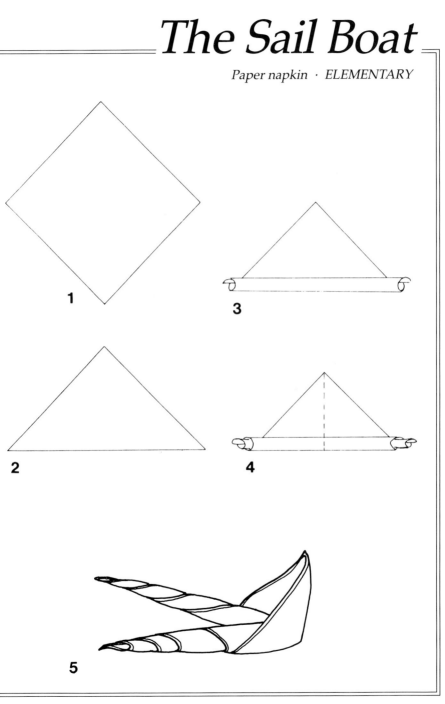

1

2

3

4

5

1 Fold the napkin into three as indicated by the dotted line and with the single edge towards you.

2 Fold corners **A** upwards as shown. Fold up the bottom edge as indicated by the dotted line. Now pleat right across the napkin from left to right, keeping the pleats vertical.

3 Open out the pleats and arrange in a glass as shown.

Bat

Paper napkin · BASIC

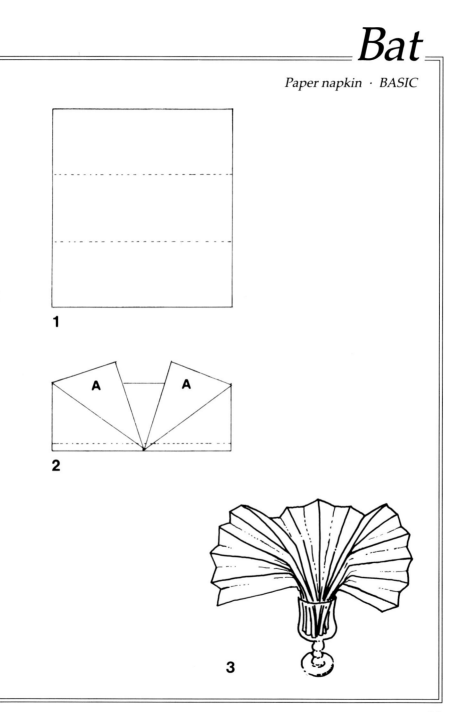

1

2

A   A

3

1 Fold the napkin into three.

2 Crease at centre line **A**.

3 Fold down corners **B** and **C** to centre line.

4 Turn the napkin over.

5 Roll **D** and **E** up tightly.

6 Fold at centre line **A**, leaving **D** and **E** on the outside.

7 Holding the napkin in the left hand by the rolled sections **D** and **E**, place the right hand inside the fold and bring point **F** down through the fold to point **G**.

8 Arrange napkin with the rolls beneath as shown.

The Scroll & Mortar

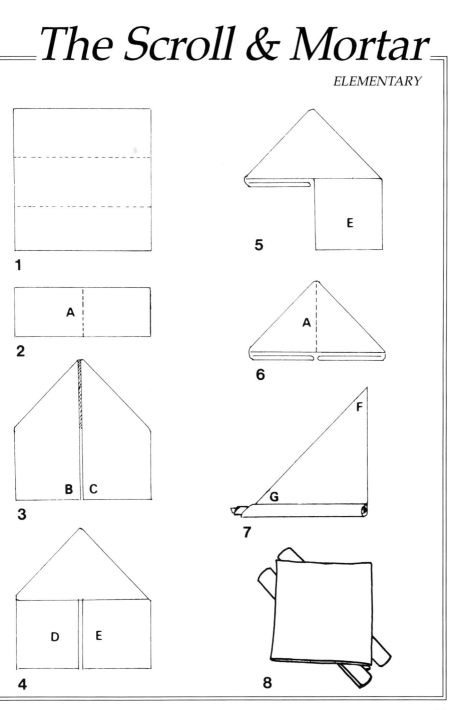

1

2

A

3

B C

4

D E

5

E

6

A

7

F

G

8

1 Fold napkin into four, ensuring that four loose edges are at **A**.

2 Fold down top flap as indicated.

3 Fold along dotted line.

4 Fold down second flap.

5 Fold second flap along dotted line.

6 Tuck second fold under first fold.

7 Fold napkin along dotted line putting the fold underneath.

8 Fold napkin along dotted line.

9 Finished fold.

Buffet Napkin Fold

Breakfast/Paper napkin · BASIC

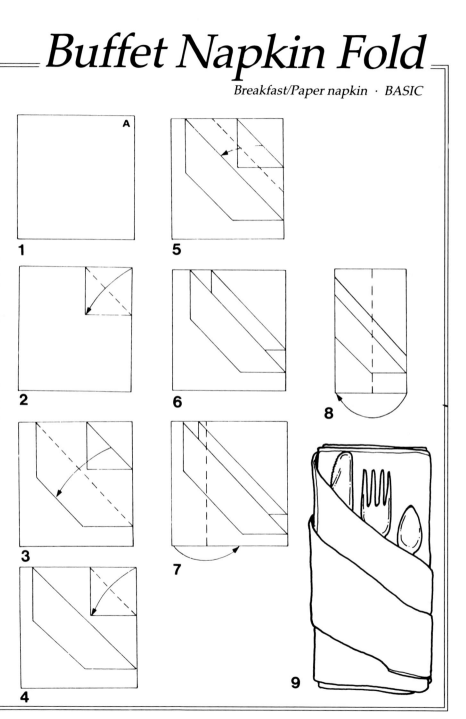

1

2

3

4

5

6

7

8

9

1 Lay napkin out flat.

2 Fold edges **A** and **B** into centre line **C**. Fold in half once more.

3 Pleat from left to right.

4 Set base of pleats in a small wine glass, open out the folds as shown.

The Single Fan

Paper napkin · ELEMENTARY

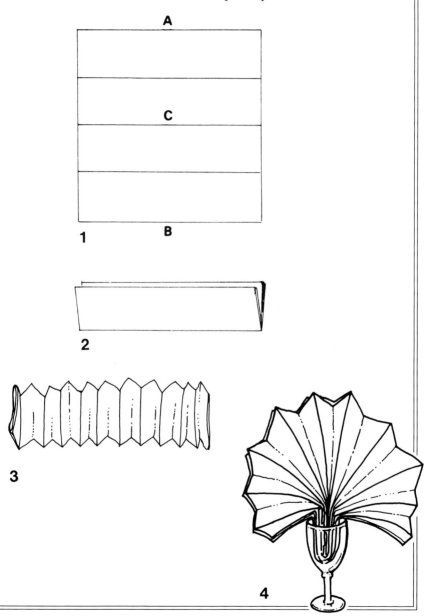

1. Fold as indicated by dotted lines.

2. Fold diagonally.

3. Turn napkin so that points are away from you. Fold sides **B** along dotted line to meet at centre **A**.

4. Turn the points of **B** under.

5. Fold along the centre line **A** and stand the napkin with fold uppermost.

6. Pull up the four pleats and arrange to produce the Finished Fold.

Cock's Comb

Paper napkin · BASIC

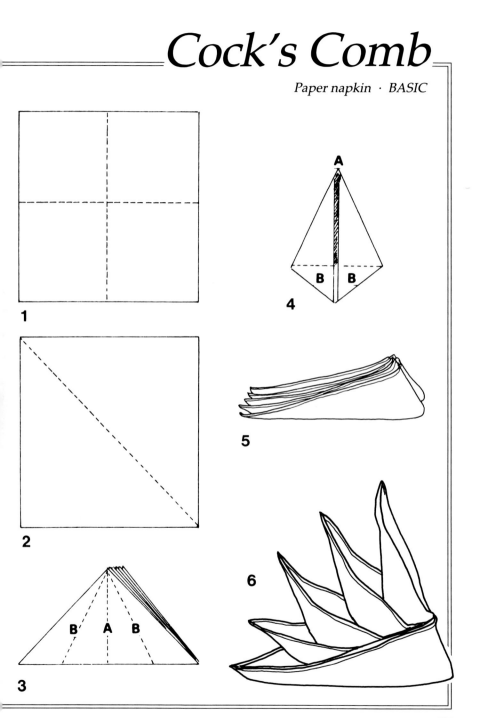

1

2

3

4

5

6

1 Fold the napkin in half,
then in half again to form a
square. Turn the napkin to
form a diamond shape.
Fold point **A** to point **B**.

2 Fold along the dotted line,
1 inch below the centre,
taking point **A** to the top.

3 Fold in half along the
dotted line and then stand
on the table.

4 Finished Fold.

The Slide

Breakfast/Paper napkin · ELEMENTARY

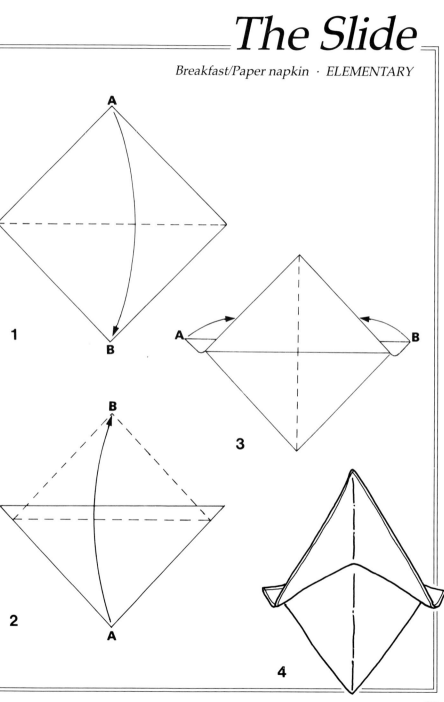

1   Lay out the napkin as a
    diamond and fold in half
    along dotted line **A**.

2   Fold the napkin along lines
    B, C and **D, E** leaving a
    space of 2 inches (5cm)
    between the inside edges.

3   Napkin after stage 2.

4   Fold up a 2 inch (5cm) hem
    as shown by the dotted
    lines in diagram 3. Now
    pleat from left to right
    across the napkin.

5   Set the base of the fold in a
    napkin ring or glass, open
    out the folds and arrange
    as shown.

Palm Leaf

Paper napkin · BASIC

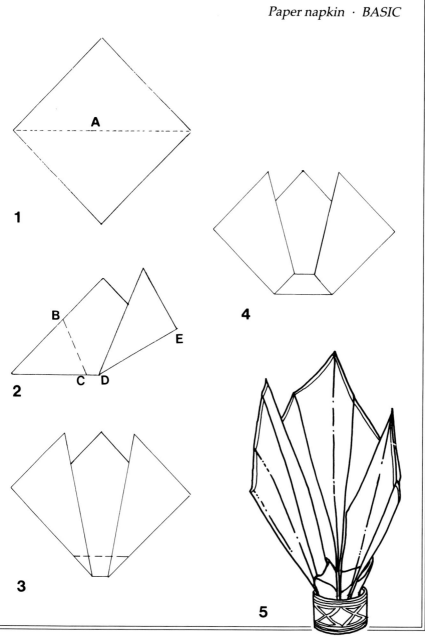

1

2

3

4

5

1 Fold the napkin in half.

2 Fold corners **A** to **B** and **C** to **D**.

3 Fold the top back at the dotted line.

4 Turning the points to the top, bring the left-hand corner round and tuck behind the front flap.

5 Napkin after stage 4.

6 Turn the napkin around and repeat stage 4.

7 Finished Fold.

The Bishop's Mitre

Paper napkin · BASIC

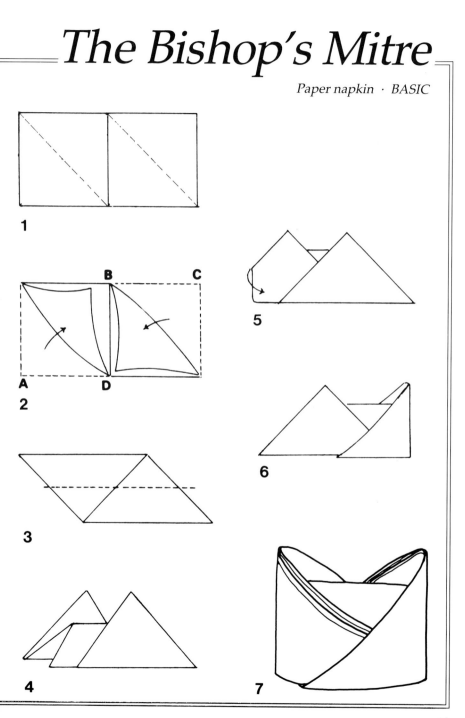

1

2

3

4

5

6

7

43

1 Lay napkin out flat.

2 Fold as indicated.

3 Lay napkin with edge **A** towards you, and pleat from left to right.

4 Secure the base of the pleats in a napkin ring and arrange pleats as shown.

Peacock Fan

Breakfast/Paper napkin · BASIC

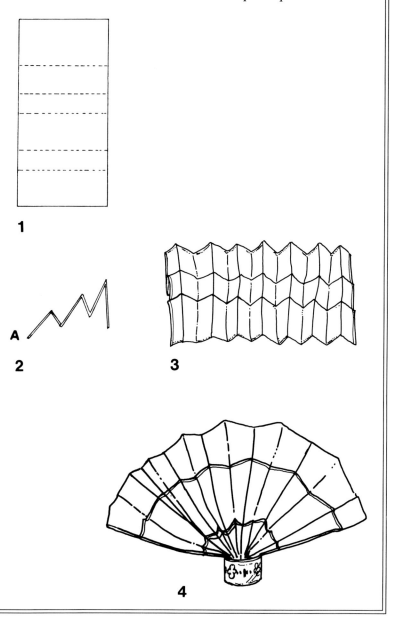

1

A

2

3

4

1 Fold the napkin into three.

2 Fold corners **A** and **B** upwards to centre line.

3 Fold corner **C** to **D** and **E** to **F**.

4 Place fingers of left hand inside fold and turn down point **GH** at the dotted line to form a cuff.

5 Mould the napkin into a cone and set on the table with the points of the cuff facing the diner.

The Cone

Paper napkin · BASIC

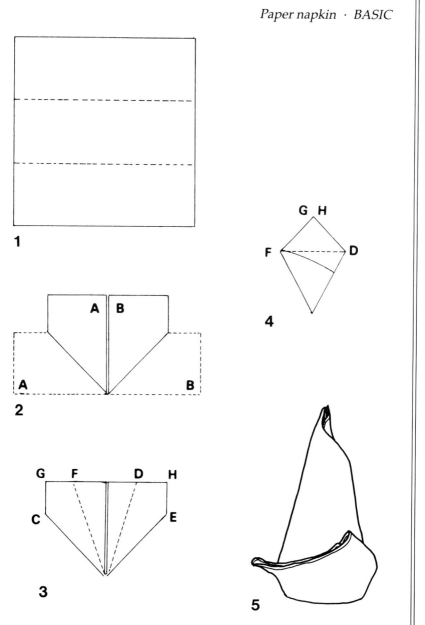

1

2

  A B

A   B

3

G F   D H

C   E

4

G H

F   D

5

1 Fold the napkin in half then in half again.

2 Fold corners **A** and **B** along the dotted line to centre line **C**.

3 Turn the napkin over.

4 Roll corners **A** and **B** outwards as shown.

5 Fold corners **A** and **B** to the top along the dotted lines.

6 Napkin after stage 6.

7 Turn napkin over. Arrange on the table with the point towards the diner.

BASIC

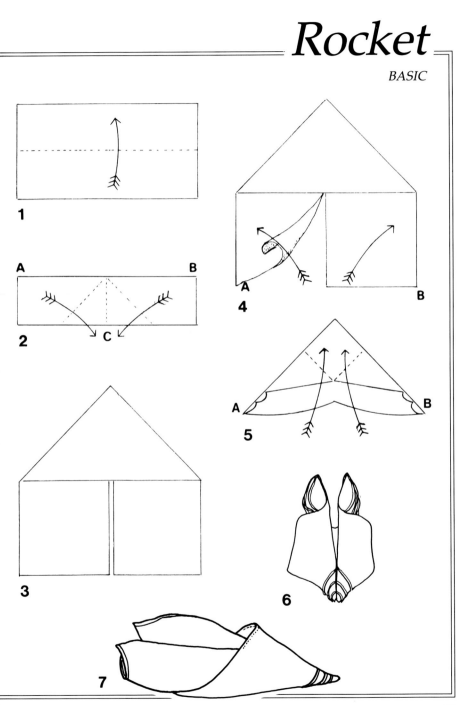

1

A   B

2   C

3

4   A   B

5   A   B

6

7

1 Lay napkin flat fold at line **A**.

2 Fold corners **A** diagonally to centre line **B**.

3 Fold corners **C** diagonally to centre line **B**.

4 Fold corners **D** diagonally to centre line **B**.

5 Napkin after fold 4.

6 Now shape fold as the completed drawing.

A better result can be obtained by using a very stiff napkin or by placing foil on the napkin at diagram 1.

The Duck

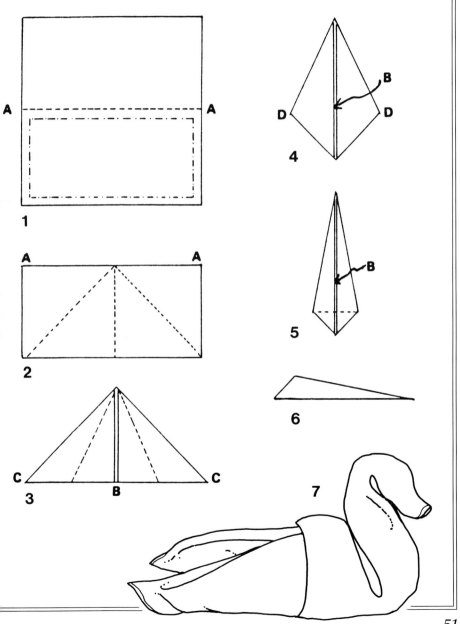

1

2

3

4

5

6

7

1　Fold along the dotted lines and place napkin with points **B** away from you.

2　Fold up the base edge 8 inches (20cm).

3　Now fold base edge back to the bottom.

4　Pleat from **C** to **D**.

5　Napkin after stage 4.

6　Separate the two layers of the pleats at the base, place the inside pleats in a glass and arrange the outside pleats neatly at the front and fold corners **A** to the back of the glass.

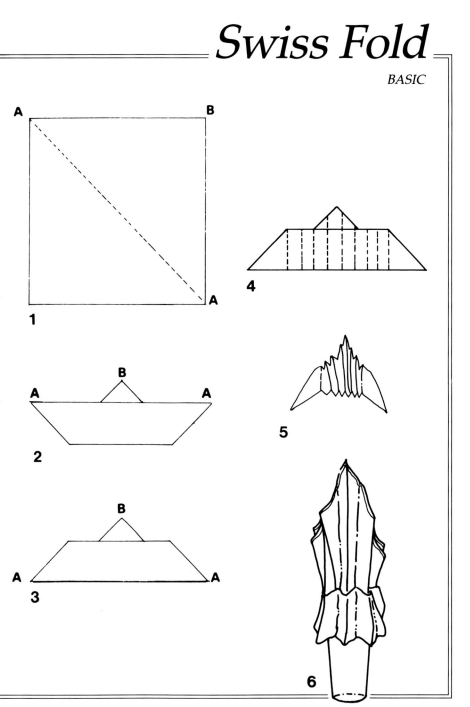

1 Fold the napkin in half to form a triangle.

2 Fold the points to the rear along the dotted line as shown.

3 Pleat the napkin right across from left to right.

4 Open out the pleats and arrange in a small glass or a napkin ring.

The Fleur-de-lys (1)

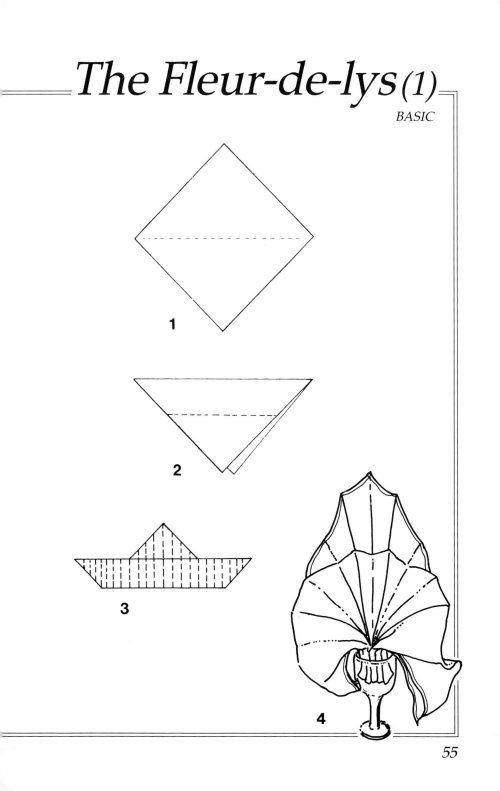

1 Fold the napkin into four equal parts.

2 Fold **A** in to centre line as shown.

3 Now fold **B** to match **A**.

4 Fold under the front corners of **A** and **B** diagonally.

5 Lift folds **A** and **B** and support on the turned back corners to create the wings. Place on the table with the points facing the diner.

Paper napkin · BASIC

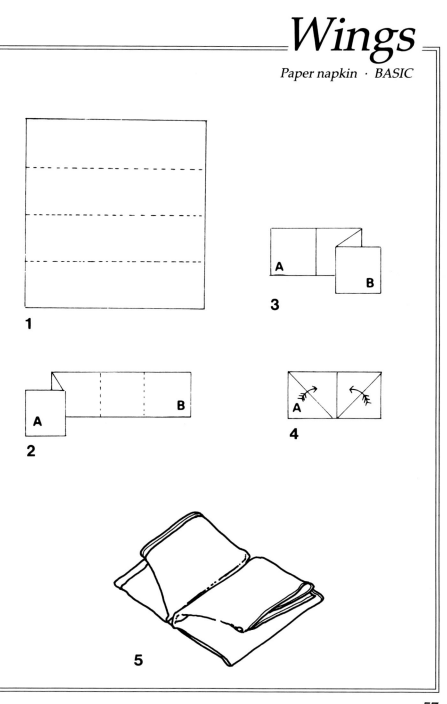

1

2

3

4

5

1 Fold the napkin in half along the dotted line to form a triangle.

2 Fold the points back on either side along the dotted line.

3 Pleat the napkin right across from left to right.

4 Open out the leaves and arrange in a small glass or napkin ring, as shown.

The Fleur-de-lys(2)

Paper napkin · BASIC

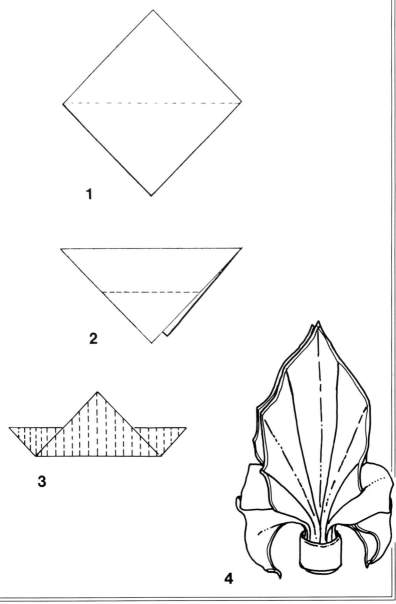

1

2

3

4

1 Fold the napkin at the dotted line.

2 Fold corners **A** up at the dotted lines.

3 Fold **B** up at the dotted line.

4 Fold **B** down at the dotted line.

5 Napkin after stage 4.

6 Turn napkin so that side **C** to **D** is away from you. Fold corner **C** as shown. Fold corner **D** up at the dotted line and tuck into the pleat at **C**.

7 Stand the napkin on the table with point **E** up.

8 Pull down the pleats to produce the Finished Fold.

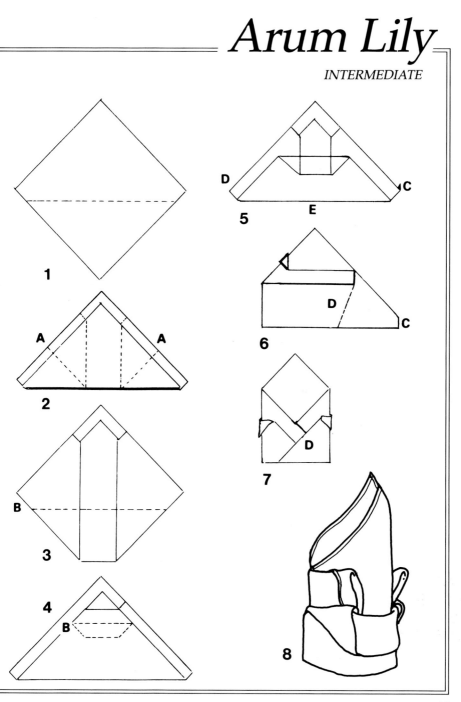

1

2

A   A

3

B

4

B

5

D   C

E

6

D

C

7

D

8

1 Fold along the dotted line to produce a triangle.

2 Fold again on the dotted line.

3 Fold **B** down on to **C** along the dotted line.

4 Pleat the napkin right across from left to right.

5 Open out the pleats and arrange the napkin in the glass as shown.

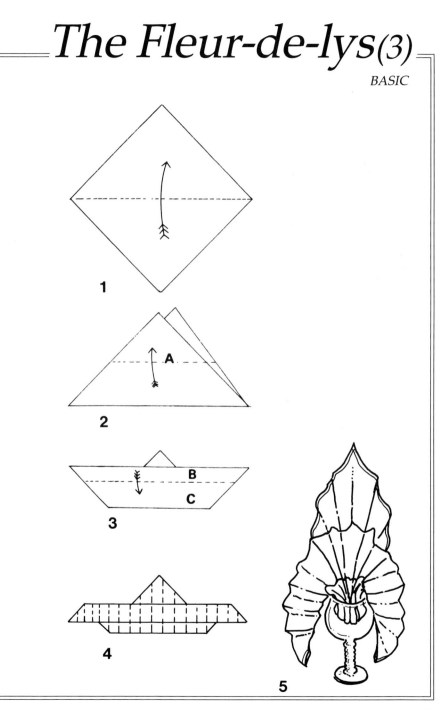

1

2

3

4

5

1 Lay the napkin flat.

2 Fold edges **A** and **C** to centre line **B**.

3 Crease as shown by dotted line.

4 Fold out the 4 corners diagonally.

5 Tightly roll from the top to the centre line. Pleat the remainder.

6 Fold in half as shown.

7 Arrange in glass. This fold may be decorated with a sprig of holly at Christmas.

Candle Fan

Paper napkin · INTERMEDIATE

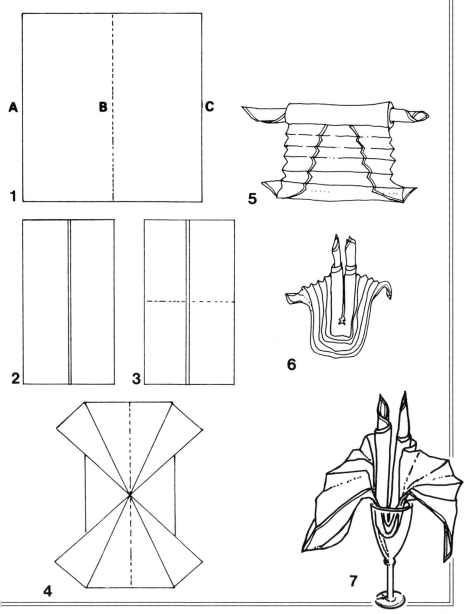

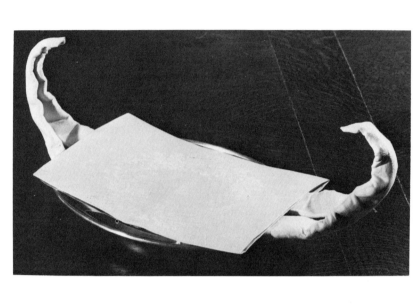

1 Lay napkin flat, cover half with greaseproof paper or kitchen foil. Fold at line **A**.

2 Fold corners **A** diagonally to centre line **B**.

3 Fold corners **C** diagonally to centre line **B**.

4 Fold corners **D** diagonally to centre line **B**.

5 Napkin after fold 4.

6 Turn napkin as shown, hold firmly with left hand and at 1 inch (25mm) intervals, pull the point up to produce fold as shown in sequence 7.

7 Finished Fold.

8 Two such folds may be joined by using a third napkin, as shown, to produce a complete Gondola.

The Gondola

Paper napkin · BASIC

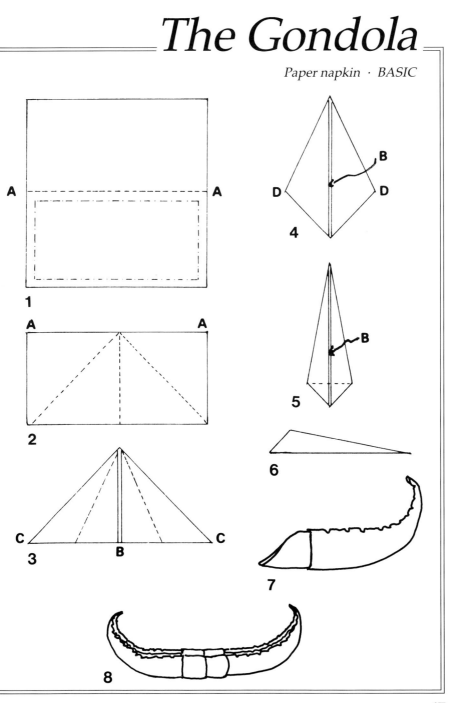

1 Fold napkin into four, ensuring that four loose edges are at **A**.

2 Pick up one flat at **A** and fold to **B**.

3 Pick up **A** and put to **B** folding at dotted line.

4-6 Repeat stage 3, folding in the direction of the arrows.

7 The underneath view.

8 Turn the napkin over so that the pleated fold is pointed from top to bottom.

9 Fold the napkin into a triangle, tuck in the edges at the back and stand with the fan facing the diner.

Norwegian Glacier

Breakfast napkin · *INTERMEDIATE*

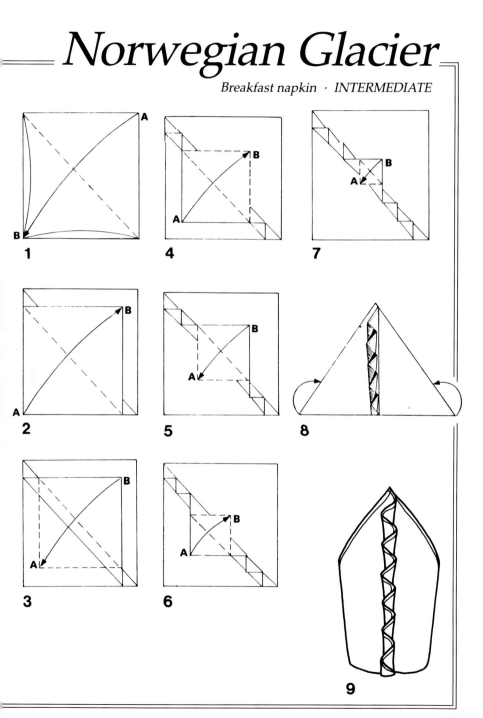

1

2

3

4

5

6

7

8

9

1 Fold the napkin into three.

2 Turn down top edge twice making a 1 inch fold.

3 Turn napkin over.

4 Fold corner **A** to centre **B**.

5 Fold **C** down and attach bow tie.

6 Fold **D** at dotted line behind.

7 Fold **E** at dotted line.

8 Open fold **D** and **E** this will help the napkin stand upright.

INTERMEDIATE

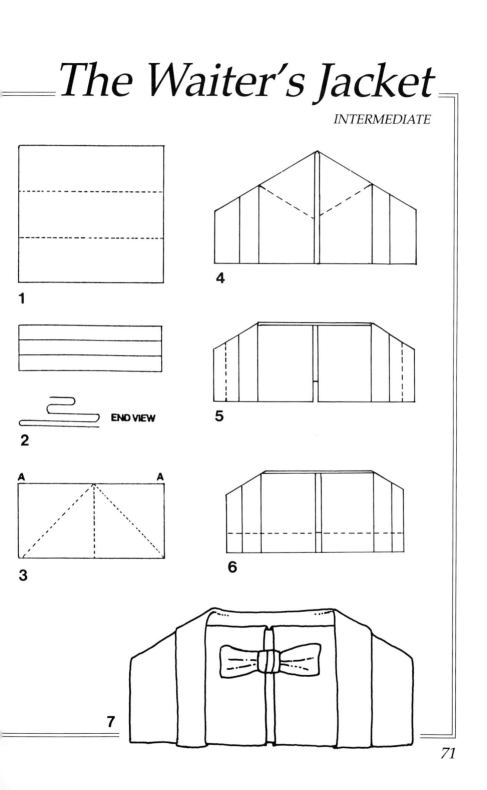

1

2

END VIEW

3

A

A

4

5

6

7

1. Lay the napkin flat and fold along dotted lines, bringing points **A** to point **B**.

2. Fold **A** to **B**. This will give a 'W' effect if viewed from the end of the napkin.

3. Pleat the napkin making 2 inch (5cm) pleats.

4. Hold the napkin at the bottom bringing points **A** and **B** together.

5. Open the pleats and pull down one side.

6. Turn the napkin round and repeat stage 5.

7. Open the napkin into a fan shape and stand on the place setting.

Oriental Fan

Breakfast napkin · INTERMEDIATE

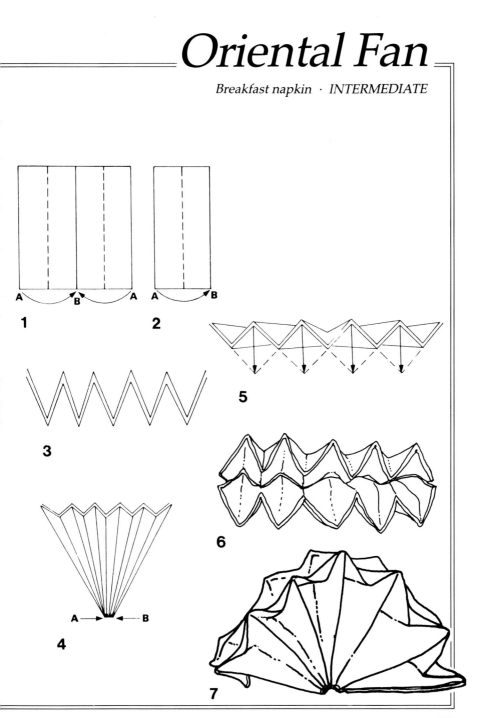

1. Fold napkin into three as shown.

2. Fold corners **A** diagonally to centre line.

3. Fold back corners **A**.

4. Keeping the two sides flat on the table, press them towards the middle; this will make the centre line stand up. Fold sections **B** under at the dotted line.

5. Open out the centre fold and arrange on the table with the point away from the diner.

The Arrow Head

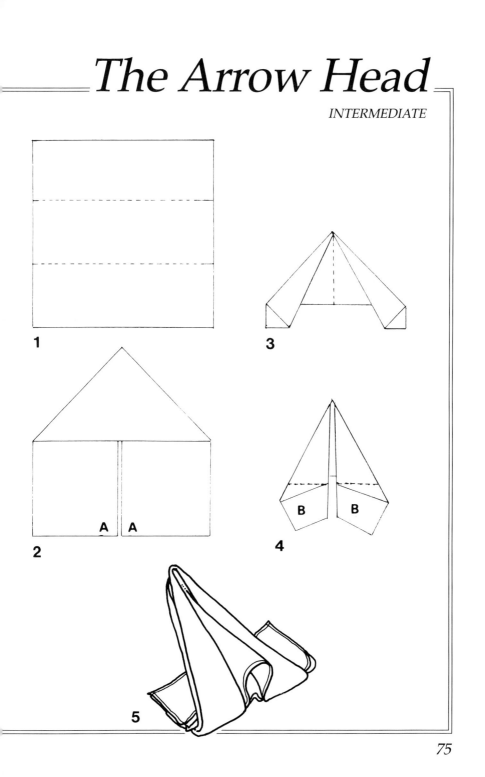

1

3

2

A   A

4

B   B

5

1 Crease the napkin and fold in four as shown.

2 Fold in half keeping the open edges towards you.

3 Fold sides inwards as shown.

4 Lift each fold and press down the centre of it to form a triangle.

5-6 Carry on until all folds have been pressed.

7 Open the folds slightly. Arrange the napkin on the table with the points of the fan away from the diner.

1

2

3

4

5

6

7

1 Lay the napkin flat and crease along the dotted lines.

2 Fold as shown.

3 Pleat the napkin from left to right.

4 Set base of the pleats in a napkin ring and open the folds, arranging as shown.

The Double Fan

Paper napkin · INTERMEDIATE

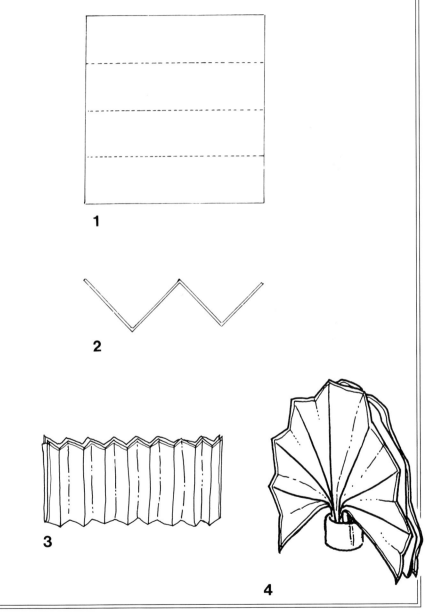

1

2

3

4

1 Lay napkin flat.

2 Fold as indicated.

3 Place napkin with base **CC** towards you and pleat vertically, from left to right.

4 Napkin after stage 3.

5 Place in a glass, bring down the front fold to expose the inside pleats, arrange as shown.

Waterfall

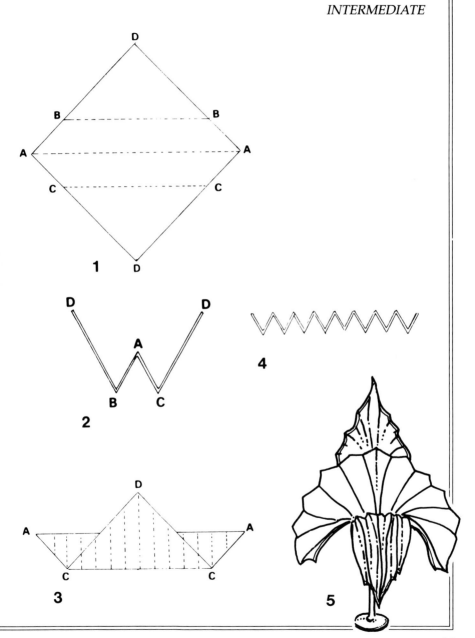

1

2

3

4

5

1 Lay napkin flat, and fold in three along the dotted lines.

2 Fold in half along the dotted line.

3 Fold corners **A** and **B** down along the dotted lines.

4 Fold corners **C** and **D** to the centre line.

5 Turn ends **A** and **B** up twice as indicated by the lines.

6 Fold in half along the centre line. Turn corners **A** and **B**.

7 Napkin after stage 6. Tuck in corner **AB**.

8 Turn napkin over and arrange on the table with the toe towards the diner.

The Elf Shoe

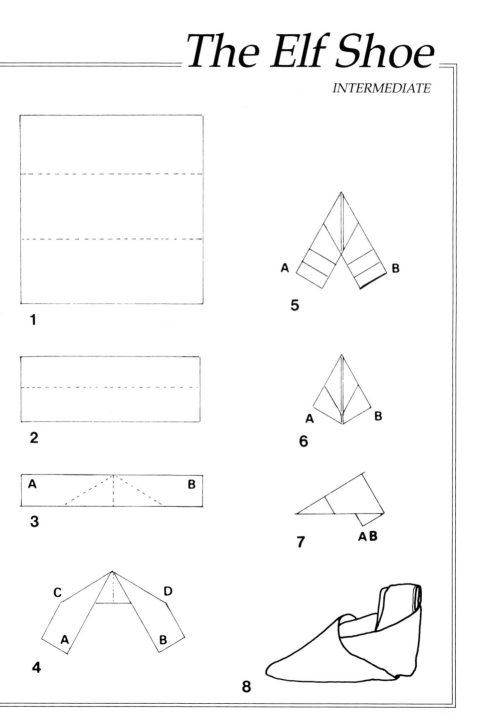

1

2

3
A   B

4
C   D
A   B

5
A   B

6
A   B

7
A B

8

1 Fold napkin into three.

2 Fold at lines **A** to bring sides **B** to the centre.

3 Napkin after stage 2.

4 Turn the point to the right, folding along the centre line.

5 Turn the napkin over, fold the portion **BB** up and away from you at the

dotted line shown in previous diagram.

6 Fold **CC** in half towards you; this will make the heel.

7 Fold **CC** around and tuck into pleat **D**.

8 To finish this fold, insert the fingers between the folds and curl this part around the slipper.

Cinderella's Slipper

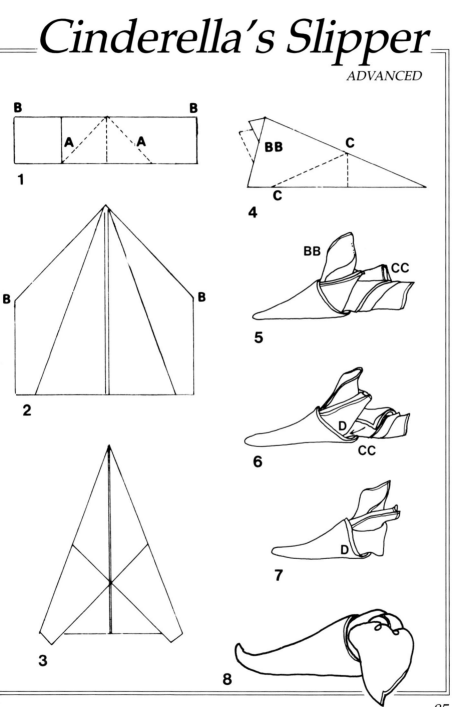

1 Lay napkin out flat, and crease along dotted lines.

2 Fold as indicated.

3 Pleat the folded napkin from left to right.

4 Set the base of the pleats in a napkin ring, open out the pleats and arrange as shown.

The Two & a Half Fan

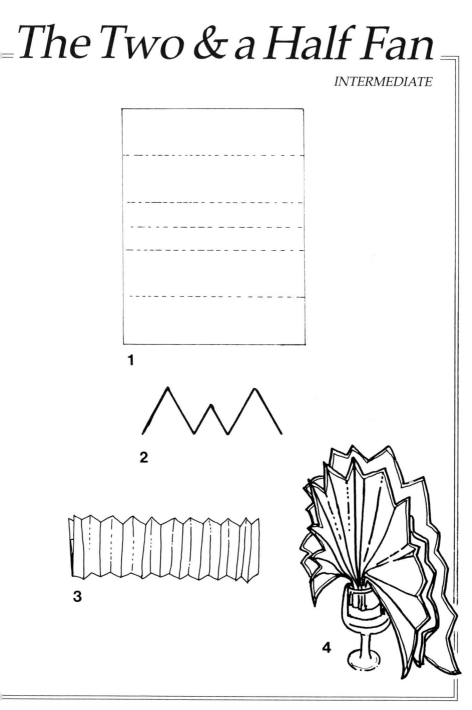

1

2

3

4

1. Fold the napkin into three equal widths.

2. Fold the top layer up one third as shown.

3. Fold in half with the pleat inside and then fold **A** to **C** and then **B** to **D**.

4. Napkin after stage 3.

5. Now fold back **E** in a diamond as shown by dotted lines in diagram 4.

6. Repeat previous fold to complete the envelope.

Envelope

Breakfast/Paper napkin · ADVANCED

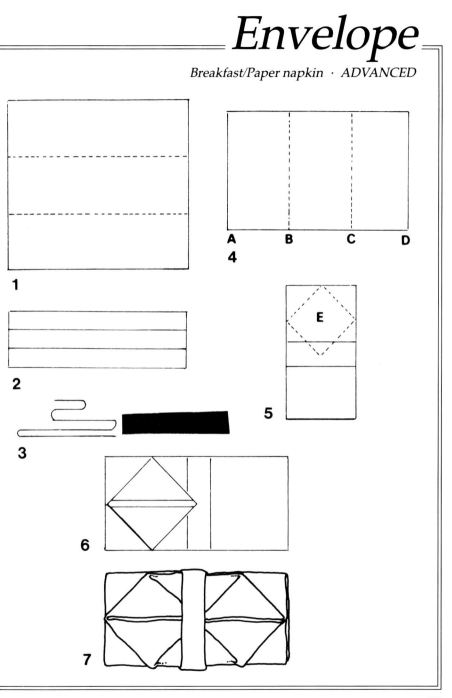

1 Fold the napkin into three.

2 Fold in half again along the dotted line.

3 Fold in sides **B** to meet at **A**. Turn napkin over.

4 Fold in corners **C**.

5 Fold the two points over along the dotted lines **D**.

6 Fold over at the centre line **E**.

7 Stand upright and arrange as shown.

8 Finished Fold.

Paper napkin · ADVANCED

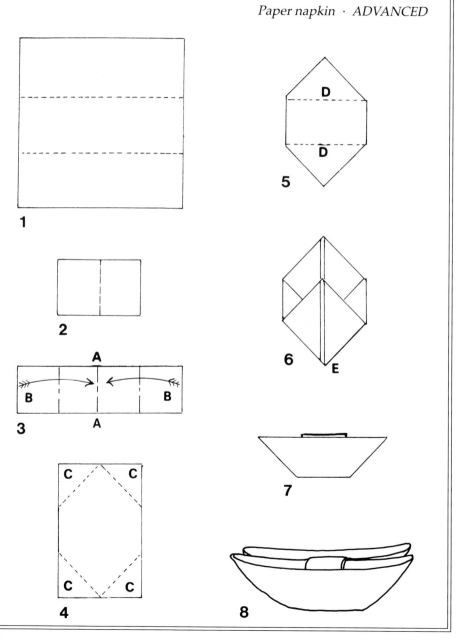

1

2

3

A

B

B

A

4

C

C

C

C

5

D

D

6

E

7

8

1   Fold the napkin into three parts as indicated.

2   Fold along the dotted lines to bring edges to the centre.

3   Fold the corners up along the dotted lines.

4   Fold the left and right corners in along the dotted lines.

5   Turn napkin over and then upside down.

6   Turn up bottom point as shown.

7   Turn the left and right corners backwards, slip one corner into the other to fasten. Open out the ears first, then the base, and stand on the place mat.

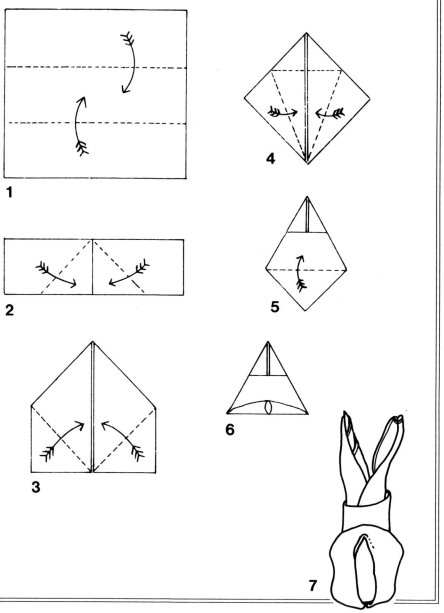

1

2

3

4

5

6

7

1   Fold the napkin into four as shown.

2   Fold the corners **A** along the dotted lines.

3   Fold the corners **D** along the dotted lines.

4   Fold the corners **D** upwards along the dotted lines.

5   Fold along the dotted lines to bring **D** over **E**.

6   Fold **F** over dotted line to **G**.

7   Fold **H** back along the dotted line.

8   Turn napkin so that point **J** is away from you, then pull point **J** right over to **K**.

9   Napkin after stage 8.

10 Open out **L** and curl the leaves to produce the Finished Fold.

The Sachet

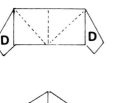

1

2

3

4

5

6

7

8

9

10

1 Lay napkin flat and fold
   along the dotted lines.

2 Turn through 45° and fold
   along the dotted lines.

3 Turn again and fold along
   the dotted lines.

4 Turn napkin over, fold
   along the dotted lines.

5 Napkin after stage 4.

6 Turn over and place a
   tumbler over the points in
   the centre.

7 Pull each of the 12 points,
   gently away from
   underneath, taking
   opposing corners in turn.

8 Finished Fold.

Rose

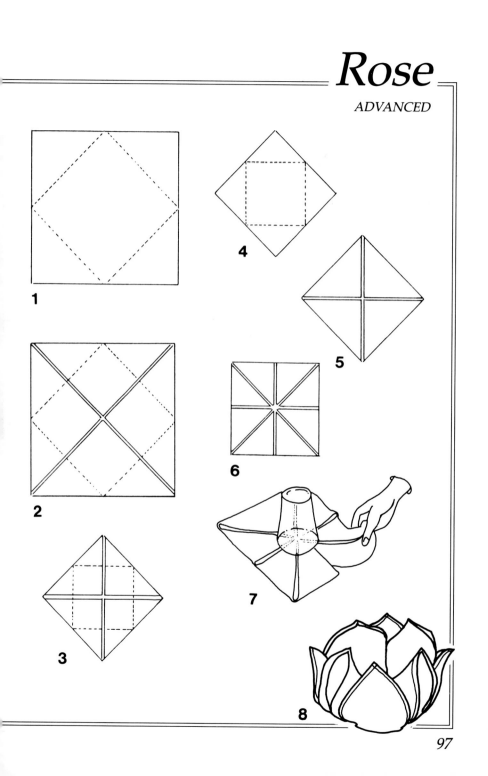

ADVANCED

1

2

3

4

5

6

7

8

1 In the shape of the duck
   this makes the head.

2 The rose turned upside
   down.

3 The lazy butler.

ADVANCED

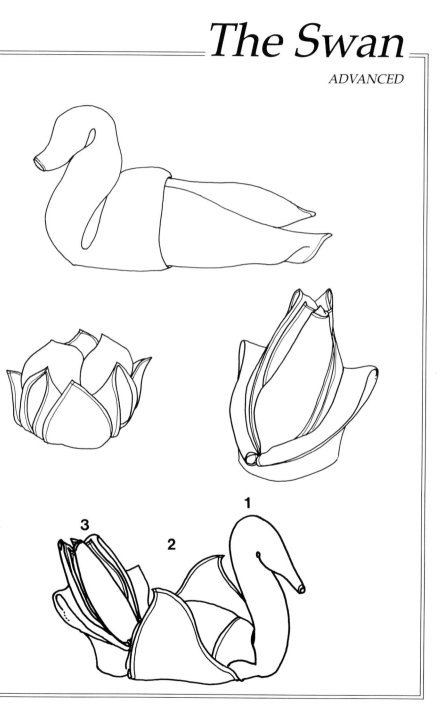

1 Fold the napkin in half diagonally then fold corners **A** to **B**.

2 Fold two flaps marked **A** up to **B**.

3 Fold the two flaps marked **A** out to the dotted lines at **B**.

4 Fold **A** to **B** ensuring that the fold falls along the bottom dotted line.

5 Fold bottom edge **A** along dotted line marked **B**, then tuck ends marked **C** around the back to make napkin stand up.

6 Finished Fold.

Viking Hat

Breakfast napkin · ADVANCED

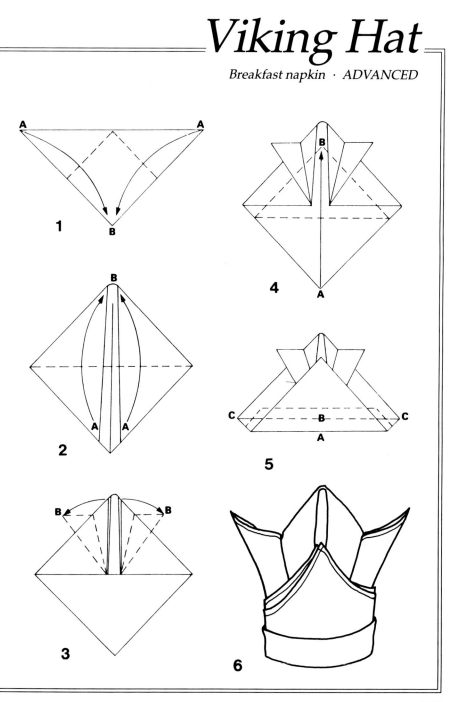

The Cockerel

INTERMEDIATE

This attractive tablepiece for special occasions consists of the Cock's Comb, Rose and Waterfall folds combined. Instructions for folding these three designs are given on pages 36, 96 and 80 respectively. The whole display relies on careful placing of the composite folds on an oval salver or board.